Jessie S. Westover

A TIME TO GROW

Copyright © Jessie S. Westover (2021)

The right of Jessie Westover to be identified as author of this work has been asserted in accordance with section 77 and 78 of the Copyright, Designs and Patents Act 1988.

All rights reserved. No part of this publication may be reproduced, stored in a retrieval system, or transmitted in any form or by any means, electronic, mechanical, photocopying, recording, or otherwise, without the prior permission of the publishers.

Any person who commits any unauthorised act in relation to this publication may be liable to criminal prosecution and civil claims for damages.

A CIP catalogue record for this title is available from the British Library.

ISBN 9781398410558 (Paperback)
ISBN 9781398410565 (Hardback)
ISBN 9781398410572 (ePub e-book)

www.austinmacauley.com

First Published (2021)
Austin Macauley Publishers Ltd
25 Canada Square
Canary Wharf
London
E14 5LQ

DEDICATION

To my sister, Angela, and to all the time we grew together.

ACKNOWLEDGMENTS

The staff at Austin Macauley who helped me grow this book.

*Seedlings planted with tender care,
given sunlight and water to share.*

*Growing slowly, starting so small,
dreaming of being big and tall.*

*Time together is a gift,
quickly dispelling any tiff.*

*Roots beginning to twist into one,
closeness shared seems forever fun.*

*Blooms are coming, it won't be long,
two flowers will sing a summer song.*

*Smiling in the sunshine, dancing in the breeze,
having each other as the only need.*

*Long days of laughter,
with twinkling night skies thereafter.*

*A storm in the distance begins to grow,
the two flowers don't seem to know.*

*Their world becomes different, dark and cold,
a storm is here that was not foretold.*

*Together fighting through a mighty blow,
having each other to support and hold.*

*Dawn is breaking only to show,
not every flower will continue to grow.*

*Damage was done,
a crooked stem for one.*

*Petals give way
with color that longs to brighten the day.*

*The harvest is here its time to show,
only one flower will go.*

*Show the world your beauty and power,
for you are the undamaged flower.*

*You'll bring a glimpse of joy wherever you go,
your destination will certainly know.*

*Autumn colors quietly appear,
giving way to a lonely tear.*

*Petals have fallen leaving just one,
standing in the late day sun.*

A single flower feeling a chill,
trying to hold strong and stand still.

The last little flower
surrendered its power.

Letting go of its seed,
as its last will indeed.

Stillness takes hold,
with a blanket soft, white and cold.

*Two flowers seemingly gone
as birds begin to spring into song.*

*Warmth is here to stay
as a new kind of sunny day.*

*Seasons have changed and now we know,
love will always grow.*

ABOUT THE AUTHOR

Jessie Westover is a wife and a mother of two young girls. She lives on a small farm in Utah where she is known as the *Farm Boss*. Her time on the farm is filled with growing and selling flowers and taking care of the animals. Farm life provides ample opportunities to teach her children lessons about life. One such lesson involves the life cycle most easily explained through flowers. When her sister passed away from cancer she was able to express their relationship and the life cycle through *A Time To Grow*.

CPSIA information can be obtained
at www.ICGtesting.com
Printed in the USA
BVHW021140040521
606425BV00011B/2605